The Back to Front World of Azzie Artbuckle

by Beth Montgomery

proudly published by

9 22000000

D1151079

First published in 2017 in England by Your Stories Matter

Story & illustrations Copyright © 2017 Beth Montgomery

www.yourstoriesmatter.org
hello@yourstoriesmatter.org

Your Stories Matter is an imprint of
Explainer HQ Ltd
Halton Mill
Mill Lane
Lancaster
LA2 6ND
England

This book is printed in the Dyslexie font, the typeface for people with dyslexia,
though we find it great for all children. Go to www.dyslexiefont.com to find out more
about the typeface.

Fonts used on the cover are courtesy of Khrys Bosland
and are available from www.dafont.com

This title is available for sale online and from loads of great bookshops.

A bulk discount is available for educational institutions and charitable organisations
through Your Stories Matter.

British Library Cataloguing in Publication Data.
A catalogue record for this book is available from the British Library.

ISBN 978-1-909320-65-9

For all the amazing people out there
who have struggled and not known why.
This is for you.

Free teaching resources

are available for this book at

www.yourstoriesmatter.org

Dyslexia is a specific learning difficulty that primarily affects the skills involved in accurate and fluent word reading and spelling. Characteristic features of dyslexia are difficulties in phonological awareness, verbal memory and verbal processing speed. *Dyslexia is not related to intelligence. As many as 3 children in every classroom could be affected by Dyslexia.*

Dyscalculia is a specific learning difficulty that primarily affects the skills involved in arithmetic, such as difficulty in understanding numbers, learning how to manipulate numbers, and learning facts in mathematics. Other difficulties include time, measurement, and spatial reasoning. *Dyscalculia is not related to intelligence. Dyscalculia can affect 1 or 2 children in every classroom.*

Dyspraxia, or **Developmental Coordination Disorder (DCD)**, is a specific learning difficulty beginning in childhood that can affect planning of movements and co-ordination as a result of brain messages not being accurately transmitted to the body. Other difficulties include memory, perception and processing as well as additional problems with planning, organising and carrying out movements in the right order in everyday situations. *Dyspraxia is not related to intelligence. Dyspraxia can affect 1 or 2 children in every classroom.*

Attention Deficit Disorder (ADD) is a specific learning difficulty having symptoms of inattention that are not age appropriate, such as appearing not to listen, being easily distracted and not finishing tasks. **Attention Deficit Hyperactivity Disorder (ADHD)** adds to this: constant movement, fidgeting, talking excessively, interrupting and intruding upon others. *ADD/ADHD is not related to intelligence and could affect 1 or 2 children in every classroom.*

Asperger's Syndrome is a developmental condition characterized by significant difficulties in social interaction and nonverbal communication, along with restricted and repetitive patterns of behaviour and interests. Children with Asperger's often find it difficult to understand how to get along with other children in their class. Sometimes they may also experience over- or under-sensitivity to sensory stimuli. *People with Asperger's are of average or above average intelligence. A few children in every school could have Asperger's.*

- It can be difficult for adults to understand how best to support neurodiverse children. So imagine how hard it is for the children themselves to identify what they need.

- These neurological conditions often co-exist, compounding the difficulties for the children.

- On top of everything else, neurodivergent children are commonly picked upon by their peers because they are different.

- It should be no surprise that stress and anxiety often go hand in hand with neurological differences, which in themselves can be debilitating. **It's not easy being misunderstood.**

Neurodiversity is a concept that embraces these neurological differences, emphasizing the different talents not just the difficulties.

While many children struggle in school because they are different from the majority, **there are many positives to being 'wired differently'**. *Did you know it is often reported that a disproportiantely large number of the world's inventors, artists and entrepreneurs are/were neurodiverse?*

We champion and celebrate these differences and encourage you to do the same with the children in your care. You can use our books and free teaching resources to get children and adults talking positively about neurodiversity.

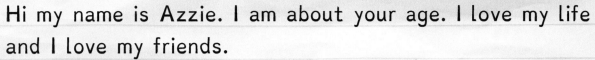

Hi my name is Azzie. I am about your age. I love my life and I love my friends.

1

At school, I would score Art and Design a big fat juicy 10 out of 10. I guess most other things would score around 5. Except Reading which gets minus 20!

Why? Because I can't read, and school is all about reading and writing. I try, I really do. But the words on the page make no sense to me at all.

I don't feel very good about myself when teachers think I'm messing around. Or when the kids in class think I'm stupid.

If I hear 'You're not trying hard enough Azzie' one more time, I think I might scream or cry.

I know that I try very hard.

I really want to be like everyone else in class who can read.
I wish people could see that.

But the more I try, the more worried I get. The more worried I get, the harder it is to make sense of the words on the page.

I can see the letters just fine, but I see them differently to everyone else.

No one believes me when I say the letters move about on the page, or look back to front. Not even my friends.

I also find it hard to sound out words from letters. And for some reason adults are always trying to get me to do that when it doesn't even help.

As for spelling, forget it! I work really hard to learn everything. Then on the day of the spelling test, it turns out I have no idea how to spell any of the words. Even though I practised hard all week to remember them. It happens every time.

You see, the thing is, I can't seem to remember spelling patterns.

Every time I see a word I have to spell it out.
It's like seeing it for the first time.
Even if I've just read that word on the same page!

So most of the time I just pretend to read and make up silly words instead.

But when I have to read out loud, I usually read the first letter of the word and make a guess at the rest of it.

12

Sometimes in class, because it takes me ages to read a sentence, the other kids get bored and finish it for me. How would that make you feel?

When it comes to doing my homework, I get so very tired.

Something that takes my best friend twenty minutes can take me all evening. Reading just one page seems to take me forever.

Once I lose interest, my mind drifts. I end up doodling on the page. Before you know it I'm off in my own dream world (again).

But I know I'm not stupid.

And everyone who knows me is always telling me I'm really smart. (Even if they don't know why I can't read.)

I know I'm good at making stuff. I've even drawn plans for shoes and had them made for my mum.

People say I have a real talent and tell me I am a 'creative genius'!

But reading makes me feel like a failure.

It doesn't help that my younger sisters have now started correcting me when I'm reading out loud.

16

GRR

I get angry at myself for being so stupid. Then I get angry at my friends because they don't understand why I am like this.

Worst of all I get angry at my mum and dad for making me try to read.

17

The harder the reading gets, the more I hate it.
The more I hate it, the more I avoid it.
The more I avoid it, the more I try to avoid school.

It usually starts at Sunday teatime. I tell them I feel sick and don't want to go to school the next day.

grumble

I argue with my mum most mornings about going to school. Sometimes it makes her cry a lot.

All this to avoid reading. Why couldn't I read? What was wrong with me?

Well one day my mum finally had enough. She decided to take me to an eye doctor to see if there was something wrong with my eyesight.

The eye doctor said my eyesight was fine.

But he gave my mum the name of a special doctor who helped kids who had difficulty reading.

OPTICIAN,

amurific

This special doctor made me take a bunch of weird tests.
The tests showed I have a 'special learning difficulty'.

We finally knew why I couldn't read!

Turns out I have Dyslexia.

It's a word that means difficulty understanding how to read words, letters and numbers.

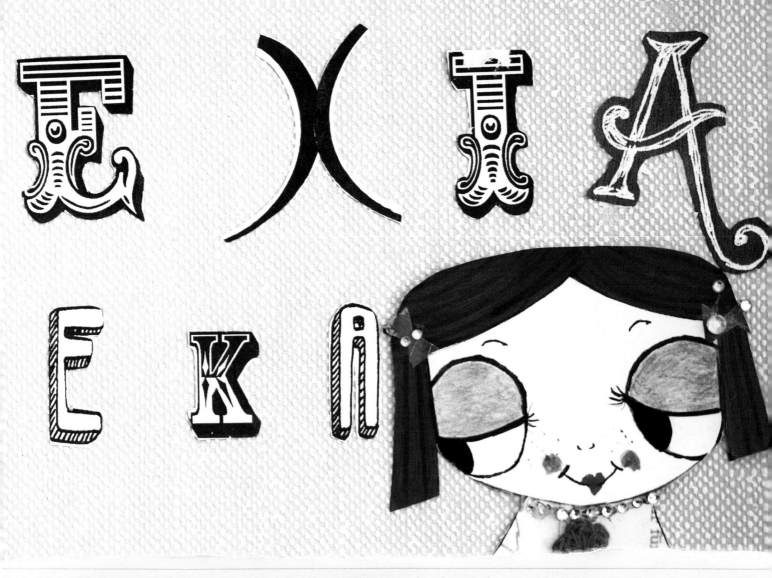

That explained why I also struggled with maths, because I found it difficult to make sense of the numbers.

Eureka! I wasn't stupid after all. I just had this special thing called Dyslexia.

At school I now get special help. I never have to read out loud, unless I am happy to.

My teachers also give me extra time on tests to understand what I am reading.

I now don't have to do all of my homework. And because it doesn't take as long, I am more relaxed and sleep better.

Guess what. This makes me concentrate better at school!

Now that they know about my Dyslexia, my friends and teachers help me a lot. It makes school so much easier!

And no one has told me off for messing about since we worked out why I couldn't read!

I've even been reading about lots of really clever people, some very famous, who struggled with reading letters and numbers: Albert Einstein, Walt Disney, Leonardo da Vinci, Alexander Graham Bell, and a really cool guy named Roald Dahl (I think he would love my drawings).
It's a pretty cool club to belong to.

28

It has taken me a long time to be proud of being me. Being different doesn't make you strange, or odd. It makes you special. It makes you stand out. It's a shame more people don't stand out.

Some other books available from
YOUR STORIES MATTER

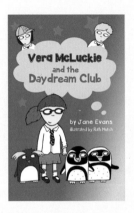

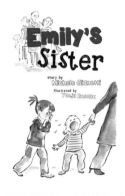

Vera McLuckie and the Daydream Club: A children's story whose main characters happen to have Dyspraxia, Dyslexia and Asperger's (not made explicit). Will relate to children aged 7-9 who feel different and left out at school. The book's real purpose is one of catalyst to help parent and teacher discuss, with children in a gentle way, what it is like to have a specific learning difficulty.

You're So Clumsy Charley: The second edition of this illustrated children's story (aged 6-8) explains what it feels like to be a child who is different from other children. Charley seems to keep getting into trouble all the time for doing things wrong. While not labelled in the story, Charley has a specific learning difficulty. When Charley learns he is not alone, things begin to get better for him.

Emily's Sister: A story told from the point of view of a child wanting to know more about how Dyspraxia and Sensory Processing Disorder affects her sister. This children's story, based on real events, paves the way for parents, teachers and medical professionals to discuss one or both of these specific learning difficulties with children (aged around 7-9).

Check them out at
www.**YourStoriesMatter**.org

Lightning Source UK Ltd.
Milton Keynes UK
UKRC02n2040170217
294704UK00003B/24